THOUGHTS OF A SILENT MIND

Hayden Bay

BookLeaf Publishing
India | USA | UK

Presentation by *BookLeaf* Publishing

Web: www.bookleafpub.com

E-mail: info@bookleafpub.com

ISBN: 9789358361681

First edition 2021

This book is dedicated to my self-made family. The people who have been there for me through it all no matter what hardships I had to face, and for my family by blood as a reminder of my love for them

Thank you

-H.B

ACKNOWLEDGEMENTS

Without my hardships I wouldn't be the writer I am today. I would have never turned to the art of writing if it weren't for every single one of you who taught me life lessons that I'll always hold onto no matter how painful they were to learn. Thank you

But in all honesty this chance I have been given to publish this book is because of my hopefully soon to be wife who found BookLeaf Publishing and believed in me enough to push me to give it a try and here we are

Thank you Bube

-H.B

PREFACE

I wrote this book because it's always been a goal of mine to get my work published and out there in some way and this is a huge accomplishment for me, I'm so proud of myself. My collection started off only being in the public eye on a Facebook page I made called "thoughts of a silent mind" which is also how my book got its name. I created this book to show the world who I am. That this silent mind indeed has a lot to say. That I'm ready for people to listen for people to hear me. So here I am

-H.B

1.

Between the sheets is where you'll find
me

Hiding from the monsters in the corners
of my mind

Grinding on a guy who's only there to be
an outlet for the rage I have inside

Rage festered up from my past, a past I
don't kindly look back on

A childhood that was anything but joy
filled

A family torn apart by poison running
through their veins

Ingested over a period of time where a
child loses track of the bottles in an
overflowing recycling bin that is so well
known to be a source of wealth for the
local homeless man who collects them
weekly

Between the sheets is where you'll find
me begging a man to ease the pain I
refuse to acknowledge

Kissing him and pretending he is the
cure for all my jagged edges

Sewing together a beautiful masterpiece
to disguise myself as a strong force to
be reckoned with, when in all truth I'd be
knocked over simply by the wind

On a foreign mattress you'll find me
laying on my back legs wrapped around
a new lover's neck as I pretend with
every stroke of his hips that my worries
wash away

one by one making me wish for it to
never end

But at a point it must come to a close
and what I was running from has never
screamed so loud

I break

I cry

I weep

And he sits beside me

Never leaving never wavering he just sits there

Doesn't hold me or place a hand on my shoulder

He just sits there and listens to my agony

Pour out

You can't keep kissing boy after boy expecting a different result.

"Between The Sheets"

-H.B

2.

Every morning you put on that fake
smile that covers your despair.

Every morning you shower away
nightmares clinging to your skin

Every damn morning you try to deny
how damaged you are

Every morning is the same

Teardrop here

Silent scream there

And the door slamming behind you as
you force your nearly frozen legs to
continue forward

You're not cold, oh God no you're just
fighting every voice in your head telling
you that you can't do this

That it's best to turn around and head
home

Every morning you stand at the bus stop hoping with everything in you that the bus just won't show up

But every morning it rounds the corner and your heart pounds in your chest

Every damn morning you can feel the panic fill you and every damn morning you can't do a god damn thing about it

Every morning it takes everything you have to not turn around and run home

Every morning the panic attacks get worse

Every morning the "what ifs" overwhelm you

Every damn morning you feel as if you will crumble

And I wish I could tell you everything is going to be okay but

Every damn morning, I feel the same

And every damn morning, I can never get it to stop   "Every damn morning"-H.B

3.

This body was born female

Even though I do not feel like one

This body was born with a chest that will one day grow even though I do not wish them too

A chest made and designed to feed and nurture a child

That I'll soon come to discover due to medical mishaps that will never become a possibility

This body was born with a stomach with extra chub

Chub with the purpose of protecting an unborn baby

This body is unique

Strong

And beautiful

This body is perfect pure and simple

This body once was a temple I mainly left empty

This body was abused

Misunderstood

And hated by me

This body has been told enough that it is not worthy by its own hand

This body has snorted one to many lines in its days

This body has ingested far too much liquor that anyone should obtain

This body has been beaten broken and abandoned all hope

This body has bleed stung and healed leaving behind a scar to remind me of what I've done

My body with the legs that allow me to walk this planet

My body with the arms to reach out for help on this earth

My body with the hands to grasp the happy moments in this life

My body I've learned to treat with respect

Because it deserves the respect it shows me from day to day

My body that I will continue to fight to keep clean

My body that sometimes aches for the sweet sweet release of a blade across its skin

My body with its twisted idea that it doesn't deserve to be feed

This body that I will feed no matter how much I believe that this body is too big for anyone to love it

That this body is just simply too ugly to gain something so beautiful and so pure as the concept of love

This body has been taken from me without my consent way more times than I can count on my own two hands

And yet my body still wakes up every day

Still takes a breath every time it gets reminded of you and shutters

Remembering what was once done to it

Remembering that fear that panic

This body I will always defend till my dying breath

Because it defends me with every cell that makes me, me

This body that hasn't given up trying to save me even when I tried to take the life it holds and protects

Loves and cherishes

This body that understands that without me there would be no it and without it there would be no me

A body that fights for me on the daily

This body that in the past I used to neglect

This body with knotted hair from two weeks of not brushing it

This body that smelled so bad yet I couldn't seem to convince myself to wash it clean

This body that I've only recently learned to love as much as it has always loved me

This body has an unconditional love for me that is simply pure

This body that has carried me up hills and mountains I never thought I could climb

This body that has faced the darkest of days and still decides to see the light

This body that I don't give enough credit to the strength and power it posses

We have a beautiful unbreakable bond

And I shall continue to learn how to unconditionally love it

As much as it does me

"An unbreakable bond"

-H. B

4.

My name is blurry face

I'm 18 years old and I have no idea who
I am

I'm a student but often feel as if I'm
learning nothing at all

I'm a human being but often feel
disconnected from the world around me

I'm a friend but often am merely a
second thought in the lives of others

I take up space but no particular reason
I go unseen in these halls

I tried my best to help others but as a
human I am also the reason some fall

I believe your most powerful weapon is
to be yourself

But it's pretty useless when you have no
idea who you are

I'm told that high school is a place to
discover who you are and often question

why it is that we judge each other along the way

I typically push everyone away but don't get me wrong, I'd be crushed if you let me go

I can be surrounded by people on all sides

And still feel completely alone

I'm a social butterfly behind a screen but get me in person and you're lucky to hold a 5-minute conversation

I am smart

But not in your traditional text book way

My mind's a dark place but give me a pen and paper and I'll show you just how beautiful the ugly truly can be

Don't call me beautiful

I really don't care

Call me intelligent

Tell me that I have something to offer

Tell me I bring joy to your day

We all do bad things and try to rid
ourselves of them

I wash my hands

But no matter how hard I scrub I can
never get them clean

I know nothing is wrong, but nothing is
right either

I'm homesick for arms that do not want
to hold me and a home that's no longer
mine

I used to love to be drunk but now I'm
hungover

When in public by myself I often sit on
my phone

Maybe because I'm bored

Maybe because I'm a teen and we are
"addicted" to them

But I like to think of it as not being a

Loser

Alone

Judged

Or anxious

Sort of a clutch

I want to live my life

But often I find myself sleeping through it all

Like a zombie

I often think about taking my own life but am too scared to try

I like to think of myself as a good-looking person but find myself using filters as much as possible in photographs

I love summer but don't even get me started on winter

What a terrible time or year

My name is blurry face

Do you know me now?

"Blurry Face"

-H. B

5.

What happens when you become the
monster you always said you'd never
be?

What happens when the prey becomes
the hunter?

The wounded becomes the abuser

The lover becomes the cold one

The selfless becomes the destroyer

What happens when you look the mirror
and see the very thing you fear the most

YOURSELF

I've spent most of my life knowing
demons live in the people who walk the
earth

I've known I had a few living in me

But I never thought they would come out
to play

In such extreme measures

I never thought I'd find myself doing the things I've done

Things I swore I'd never do

Levels that I promised myself I'd never scoop down too

And I think over the years I've been to focused on the demons living in others around me instead of my own

That needs to change

I need to change

Because I'm no better than the actions I have judged others for

I woke up screaming for a life I thought had meet its end

Sweat pouring down my face

My breath sucked out of my burning lungs

The monsters creep in the back of my mind

And I swear for a moment they come to life in the corners of the room

Hidden in the shadows as if their afraid to be seen

Watching me as I drift back to sleep

"What If?"

-H.B

6.

Darkness is a terrible thing

Makes it easy for the demons to hide

Feeding our hearts and minds with lies

Picking at us till they reach our soul

Running around, door to door, tinting our
spirit, as they roar

Ploughing through our walls of defences
as if they were only locked doors

It's not the fact that their coming for our
deepest fears and insecurities that
scares us

It's the fact that we know their coming,
we just don't know when

Maybe they're a mile away, maybe
they're just around the corner

And in the darkness the fear eats us
alive

Sometimes it's not the demons that kill
us

Sometimes the fear drives us crazy and we kill ourselves.

"When Darkness Takes Over"

-H.B

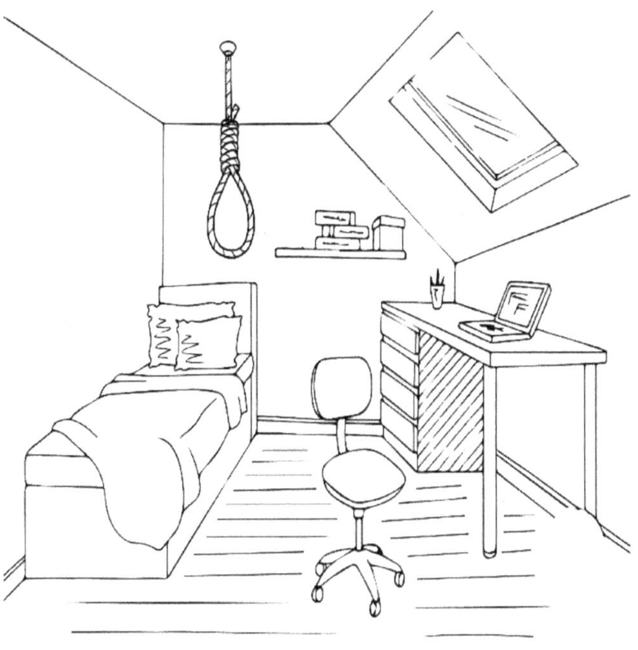

7.

Doesn't it suck? To feel completely helpless....

To just sit back and have your life drain from your body...

After being told you are unworthy

Doesn't it suck to know you're powerless...

To just lay there unable to make a difference

Doesn't it suck to know that your being over powered by me

Doesn't it suck to have the tables turn

Doesn't it suck to be looking up at me

Instead of looking down upon me

Doesn't it suck being the one torn apart from the inside

Till you can't cope any longer

Till you need a release so desperately you harm yourself

Doesn't it suck to be the one being killed

Because I've turned into the killer you once were to me

And you're my first victim

In a long line of broken hearts...

He pleaded with her to understand

Without an explanation offered in sight

Her silence is all it took

He sat there staring at her

Waiting for her to speak

He seeked anything he could get from her

She stayed silent having nothing to say

He thought he could play his silly little game and she would still hit restart

Like every time before

But this time was different

This time she was smart

This time she hit delete

And walked away with her dignity still in tact

As he sat there in defeat,

Starting a new day.

"New Beginning's"

-H.B

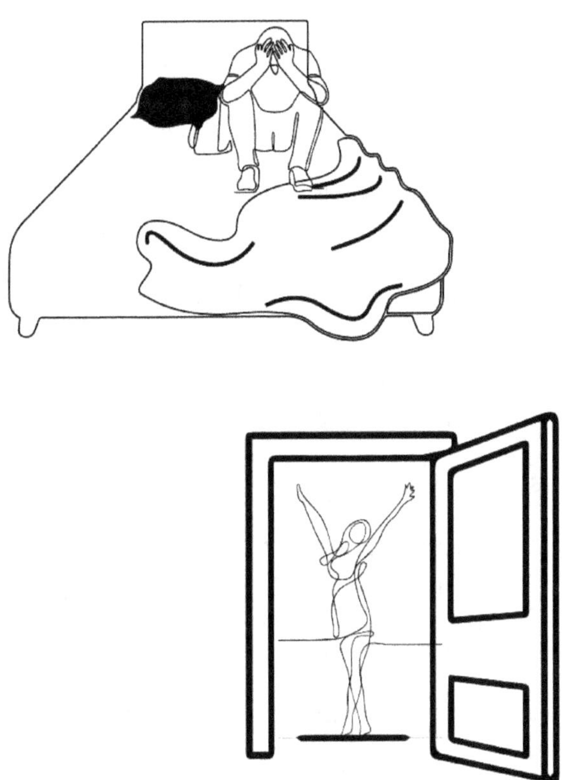

8.

Today I'm wearing bright pink lace
panties

Today under these clothes

In an attempt to take back what's mine

Under these clothes

Is where you touched me

Touched the skin of a human repeating
the word no

Under these clothes is the hole

A hole that you decided you deserved

Without permission

You decided it on your own

Under these baggy clothes

Ones that do me no justice

As everyone likes to say

I used to think that these baggy clothes that do me no favours were my safety blanket

That no one would see me that way as long as I hid under these clothes that now a days seems more like a prison

Under these clothes

You laid your hands on skin that will be forever scared

Skin that no matter how hard I scrub I can never get clean

Under these clothes is a human being that you took without a second thought

Under these clothes is a person that's damaged but not destroyed

Under these clothes lays the body that belongs to no one but me yet seems to have been taken from me over and over again

Under these clothes there's nothing

Yet everything

So tell me again

It was just a misunderstanding, right?

Under these clothes

The truth lays to rest

"Under these clothes"

-H.B

9.

Because your tough

Because your tough

Your like lightning in the sky your voice
booms like thunder

And when your down it may be stormy
weather

But that rainbow is going to stand higher
than ever

Your hallo may snap

But those two pieces make for a sharp
set of horns

And your father might have hurt you

And many men after that

Even a couple of girls at that

But ain't nobody gonna tear you down
they'll have to kill you to get that

You shine like a thousand suns on a
sunny day

My dear your beauty and might, puts the fear in men and woman alike

"Don't fuck with me tonight"

-H.B

10.

All she wanted was to be loved

All her pleas were to simply allow
yourself to love her

She cried out for you to just hold her
and accept her

To not let fear of the future stop you
from finding out how it truly ends

To not put the pen down here

But the most she could get was your
hands wrapped around her neck

moaning her name over and over again
in her ear

The only time she feels like she truly
has you as hers

And not a dream she holds onto so
dearly

All she wanted was to be loved

And boy is she gonna be loved tonight

"Broken hearts don't bleed, they beg for mercy"

-H.B

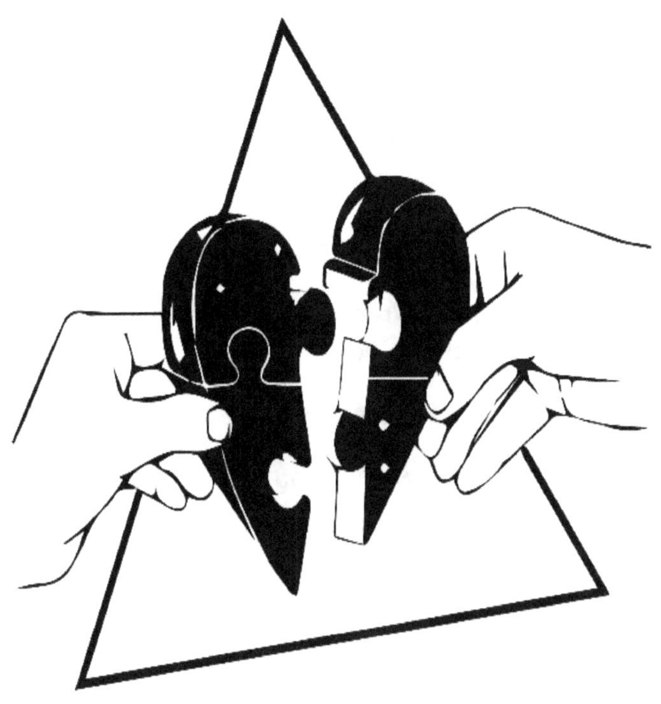

11.

I wasn't always this way

I used to be full of life and eager to walk
this earth

I wasn't always this way

I used to have such an amazing smile
that people thought was permanently
stuck on my face

I wasn't always this way

I used to love to dance and blow the
roof of this place

I wasn't always this way

And I know what you're about to say

That I still am full of life and I still have
that amazing smile and you've caught
me dancing down the sidewalk late last
summer

But these things make such rare
appearances that I truly believe I've lost
them

So, I'll say it again

I wasn't always this way

And I'm trying to find my way back to the
joy I've lost and so desperately crave

"The old me"

-H.B

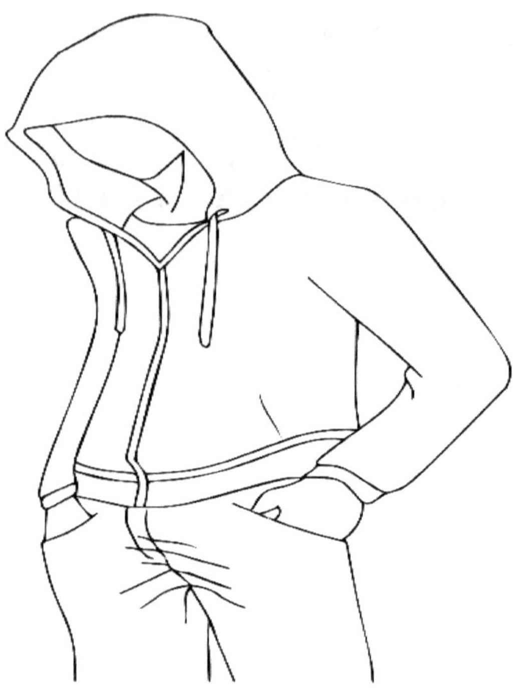

12.

In the light of day, I'm just an average teenager

I attend high school

I argue with my mother

I beg to hang out with my friends

I'm always late for dinner

But in the coverage of the night, I'm anything but... Average

One small white line leads to two

Which leads to a dozen

One glass of wine leads to the whole box

one pill leads to the bottle

One tab turns into one hell of a high that

I'm afraid to come down from

I live for the high and the freedom it brings

In the light where I cannot hide in the shadows

In the bathroom you shall find me trying to not make too much noise as I don't want my perfect picture of who I am to be shattered

This picture I've painted it's nothing short of a masterpiece

You wouldn't know the difference because you've never seen me any different

The haze is what I crave

The feeling of bliss is the road I'm on

And if I keep this up

If I keep risking it all

Just for a bit of serenity

I might find myself at a dead end I can
no longer escape from

"Dead end"

-H.B

13.

I know this won't do anything in the long run

I know that after reading this most of you will forget it and move on

But here it goes

Listen closely to the words about to be spoken

Remember that guy in the hallways with the pale skin and the cuts crawling up and down his arms

You know the one you tease for his way of coping

Have you ever stopped to wonder what's under the surface that he's hiding?

What if I told you, you were the cause of those fresh cuts on his arms?

Remember that girl with that guy

The way you envy her for her cute
relationship and hate on her for having
what you want

What if I told you, he abused her at
night?

Next time think again when you see her
in the hallways crying

Remember that guy with the so-called
perfect life

Fancy house flashy car, you know living
the high life

Have you ever seen the discoloration of
his skin?

What if I told you his parents try to shut
him up by using their fists?

Remember that girl who never says a
word

The one you pick on for the clothes she
wears or the colour of her hair

What if I told you, she's an amazing
person?

Would you believe me? Would you even care?

Remember that boy

With no light in his eyes

How you made fun of him for his taste in music you particularly don't like

What if I told you when you hear screaming, he hears meaning?

So, the next time you have something to say why don't you think before you open that mouth

Because believe it or not words actually do hurt

"Bookshelf"

-H.B

14.

Who taught you that?

Who taught you that apologizing and admitting guilt was a bad thing?

Who taught you that apologizing means you're going to get punished?

Who taught you that it's normal to beat someone when they have admitted their faults?

Whoever did that

Does not understand the concept of love

Whoever did that is dead ass wrong

Apologies are the foundation of unconditional love

Apologies are what leads to healing, and recovery

Apologies make the people we love in our life feel better after we have hurt them

Apologies leads to forgiveness

Apologies are the very glue that holds
this world together

Because we all make mistakes

It's what you do after that mistake that
counts

When we learn about apologies at a
young age that knowledge sticks with us

If the knowledge we have is correct
that's a good thing

If the knowledge we have been given is
false

We struggle with our relationships with
our loved ones

Our loved ones want to feel like their
feelings are valid

Apologies are the best way to make
someone feel heard respected and
loved

Apologies are not something to fear

They are a magical way of showing
empathy

And the gateway to greater things

And a better understanding of one
another

Whoever taught you any different is
wrong

And I will show you the true grace
apologies give to this world

The peace they bring in hearts full of
sorrow

I will show you the positive outcomes
that apologies can provide

You will learn my darling and I'll be here
to guide you on to the right path

I love you

"Who taught you"

-H.B

15.

I'm homesick for arms that don't want to hold me

I crave lips that's don't belong to me

Here I am completely and utterly in love with you

While your moved on and happy with her

Without me

And I don't know why I'm so madly in love with you

It's been so long after all

But I can't help myself

You will surely be the death of me

I miss you

I crave your laughter after I tell a joke

I want to be the one you look for in a crowd

Your voice soothes me like a lullaby
does a child

I want to feel the touch of your skin like I
once have

But all I have is you in my dreams

It's all fun and games

Till I wake up

And the torture of not having you hits
me deep

I can't scrub the memory of your touch
off of me

"I'm homesick"

-H.B

16.

1930

Were the numbers etched into the wood
beside my head

1930

Was it a set time on a clock?

Was it a year back in the day?

Was it how many minutes someone had
spent within these four walls that are
right now in this moment holding me?

Or perhaps days

Is it the number someone repeats over
and over in order to remain calm?

Is it the street number someone once
lost their innocence in?

Or possibly the exact moment someone
was left heartbroken?

Maybe even the time stamp on
someone's time on this earth….?

1930

I lay here for hours

Locked in this room

Staring at the notes carved into the
wood left behind by those who came
and went before me

Some were dark yet I drew comfort from
their darkness

I related to what others had trapped in
their minds

Their twisted thoughts

And warped views on reality was
appealing to me

Note after note

Some etched over top of others

But my eyes always fall back onto

1930

Was it the code to the last shelter
someone was staying at and they
needed to remember it to get back in?

Was it the age gap between oneself and one's abuser?

1930

1930

1930

It buzzes around my head echoing off the walls of my mind

The endless possibilities

The stories 1930 could tell

Because it keeps me busy

Keeps my mind thinking about other stories besides my own

Keeps me safe

Keeps me warm

Keeps me sheltered

Keeps me sane as the hours go by all so slowly

"1930"

-H.B

17.

I understand we both grew up in a
different time

a different view of the world

 and sometimes what feels like an
entirely different universe

I understand that you were raised in a
generation of silent woman with their
tails tucked between their legs watching
every word they spoke as to not wake
up the beast that lives within their man

A man that's supposed to love them

I understand that in your childhood you
were taught that mental illness isn't real
while watching your mother talk to and
see things that were not there

I understand that me and you are not
the same

You were only bullied at school for me
they followed me home on a screen that
fits in my pocket yet never seems to
leave my hands

I understand that for you Leaving home was a huge accomplishment

Get married

Buy a House

Go to college

Make a home out of that house by making a family to live in it

A free life

For me it's a broke life

An I'll never own my own house type life

A take more than half my monthly wages for an apartment that will never truly be mine type life

A sure I could go to college but who could afford it type life

A student loans debt creeping on my shoulder for years to come because I still have bills to pay

Mouths to feed

And a life to live

On-top of all that debt that never seems
to stop screaming off in the corner of my
mind

A why would I bring a child into this
world that only wants to kill you the
moment you take your first breath type
life

I understand that for you this world was
once covered in trees as far as your
eyes could see

I understand that animals going extinct
was never a possibility in your minds

I understand that affording enough food
for a month wasn't ever a fear in your
household

I understand that pollution was the last
thing on any of your minds when
scientists cooked up cheaper ways of
making it so we can live our privileged
lives

You only saw a gold mine

I understand how the leaders in your
generation never thought about the
future

Done the math

Or even stopped to consider

Maybe the earth is more important than
fattening your wallets

Why is it that our generation has to
repair all the damage you have caused?

And yet some of us were raised by you
and still are blind to the cause

How dare you pollute our oceans so
much they mainly consist of plastic

How dare you make the air we breathe
toxic to inhale

How dare you clear-cut jungles,
rainforests causing floods to take out
our homes

How dare you destroy every ecosystem
you lay your eyes on

Only thinking about the artificial profit
and not the legitimate reality of the
negative impact we make on our plant
that only ever tries to be there for us

How dare your leaders have children
only to corrupt their souls at such a
young age it's hard for anyone to
unlearn it as they get older

Now us humans on the bottom of the
food chain

The ones who work none stop and
provide for our leaders

The ones who don't earn enough or
have medical insurance at their jobs

The ones packaging those boxes and
working crazy hours

The ones having three jobs because
that's the only way to pay the bills

The ones protesting and showing how
angry we truly can get

Because this world needs a change

I'm sorry and I understand your
hardships and struggles but it's time to
fix the damage we have done as a
human race

Because the earth doesn't need us

It can do just fine without us

But we need HER

Simple as that

"#ReparentYourParents"

-H.B

18.

The voices in my head be screaming so
damn loud

And I don't know if there's any way to
block them out

They tell me I'm worthless they tell me
I'm too far gone

They tell me I will never make it

They tell me I'm doomed to fail

They tell me I should be grateful

Living pay check to pay check

Because at least I have a home

Money

A chance

But what they don't seem to understand
is that I know what it feels like to only
know the streets as your home

And I am forever grateful that I do not
live in that darkness anymore

But that does not mean I do not fear returning to that way of life again

Every time we're down to our last 25 cents

I fear that next month we won't be able to pay my phone bill

Or internet

Or God save our souls

The rent

I know I'm lucky to live pay check to pay check

I know there are other not as Fortunate

But this life still isn't easy

When the bank has nothing but 25 cents in it with a week left to go in the month

On top of that let's not forget the 500 dollars on that credit card

This shit is hard

This world is so full of greed and ignorance that the people in power don't care about the people who feel like they

have no control over their own lives
what so ever

People look down on me because I'm on
disability

They say "you don't deserve my taxes"

"Your just lazy"

"That's just a free pass at life"

But what they don't see nor understand
is that mentally I can't work a 9 to 5

5 days a week

What they don't understand is that I
become mentally so unstable I have to
put myself in the Psych Ward and either
quit my job or loose it because

they don't think I can handle it either

And I understand we pay a lot of taxes
but I can't simply live off $1200

When rent for a shitty small apartment is
$1600

Because we couldn't find anything
cheaper

I understand you may think nothing of
me

But if a murderer is granted shelter food
water and basic human hygiene

Then why aren't we

"Crush the stigma, eat the rich"

-H.B

19.

When I think of you

When I think of you, I feel nauseous

When I think of how I let you control me

I typically start to hate myself

I feel guilty

I have remorse

Yet still when things get tough, you're
the first thing I think of

You're the first place I want to visit

You're a dark place filled with regret and
pain

Yet you bring so much comfort and
peace in the moment

The numbness you provide is my
escape from this world

You are a monster that follows me
around day by day

You are addiction

You are my safety blanket I held onto like a child

You first showed your face disguised as Molly

Then you changed your appearance to cocaine and acid

And when I finally escaped those three costumes you have worn

You hid your ugly face behind alcohol

But no matter what costume you wore it will not change the fact that you are addiction

I've been on the path to recovery for nearly 3 years and you would think the longer I go without tasting your numbness the more I'd forget about you

But that is false

No matter how long I go without caving into you

You will always be here

Feeding me with the idea that you'll take away all the pain

I feel guilty

 I'm afraid of what dead end you might
lead me too

Yet I still really desperately want to rely
on you

And I'm ashamed

"Ugly friends"

-H.B

20.

The wind speaks to me

The wind speaks to me through the tussle of the leaves scattered on the ground

The sun speaks to me telling me tales so full of light it's nearly as warm as its rays beaming down on my pale skin

The clouds tell stories because they come in different shapes and sizes

Telling stories of giants in the sky

Rivers roar as the water smashes against the rocks reminding me of his pounding voice yelling at me to provide more

The rain falls bouncing off the cement washing away the muddy footprint that used to be there

Reminding me of healing, growth and the feeling of your worries and problems washing off your skin and down the drain

The thunder reminds me that while
doing so it's okay to cry

Butterflies flutter and so do the birds

I listen to them sing to me

And I wonder what have they seen

What stories have they been told

For my stories on the ground could not
compare to theirs up in the sky

The knowledge they must possess

The wisdom

I wish to have that one day

But for now, little chickadee

I'll listen to your stories

And hope that one day I grow up to be
like you

Strong free and adventurous

"Free Bird"

-H.B

21.

Sometimes I feel like a Gay turtle

Hiding in my shell away from the
religious view of my homophobic family

A gay turtle who carefully picks and
chooses when to show their true colours

Colours so vibrant it would blind their
holy eyes

But to my friends and my chosen family
those colours are gorgeous

And I feel like a gay painted turtle

Nervous to be me but nevertheless
wears their true colours on their back
trying to stand tall

Proud

But there will always be those moments
where I must remove my gay flag and
hide it in my shell

For I'm too afraid to have these
conversations where all they do is try to
tell me I'm wrong

That my love is a sin

That they love my fiancée as a person

But don't love her as my anchor

My person

My lover

So, I shelter and hide my gay turtle

My shaking scared head slides outta my shell

Waiting to be attacked for just existing

But I do not dare wear my pride on my back

I do not dare rub my gayness, my utterly beautiful love in their face

Outta fear they will attack me

Outta fear I will feel ashamed of the love I feel

That I will feel ashamed that I will never give them the marriage that they prefer

That I will never feel comfortable to wear my rainbow with pride again

That they will make me fear my love

Like they once have

"Gay turtle"

-H.B

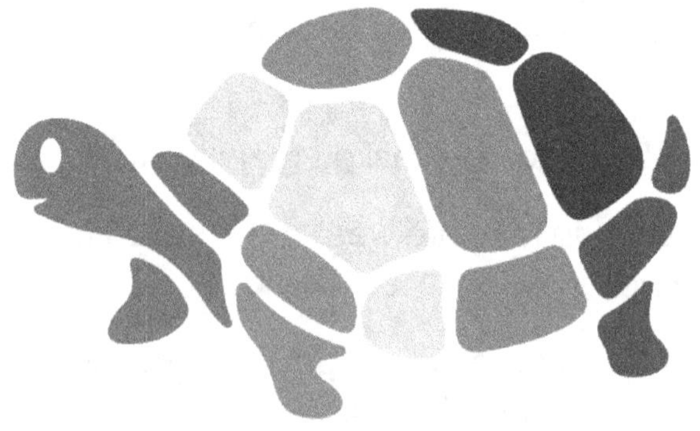

22.

I miss imagining your face

What it would look like

What colour your eyes would be and how they would glitter in the sun on a Monday morning

I miss thinking about the adventures we would go on together

I miss going to Parks and listening to all the children's laughs and wondering which one you'd sound the most alike

I miss looking at their faces and outta curiosity think about what yours would look like

I miss picking a child up after they had fallen down and knowing one day, I'd do the same for you

I miss holding a stomach that was no longer recognizably mine knowing it was stretched to contain a life that would one day bring another into this world

I miss the few precious moments we shared

Singing you songs, playing you Radiohead

I miss everything you never got to do

I miss the feeling of you growing inside of me

And how I used to wonder what you'd grow up to be, a doctor, a nurse, a stripper, an astronaut, a plumber, teacher, diver, magician, firefighter

The endless possibilities

All come with different lives to be lived

Endless possibilities that only were proven to indeed have an end

the fact you never came to be in this world

You never took your first breath

Yet I miss you

I miss you and the life we could have shared

I just wish I could hear your laugh just once

I wish I could have heard your very first cry in this life

And mamma wants you to know my baby

That just because you can't cry doesn't mean I won't shed those tears for you

And with every day that goes by I'll miss you

Deeply, honourably, and with great sorrow

"I miss you"

-H.B

23.

Your unaware of the fact she's not
breathing

 has anyone told you she's dying?

Has anyone told you you're strangling
her?

Look at her

The life slowly draining out of her body

Her eyes growing duel, the light melting
away from her golden-brown eyes

You're killing her

Your words like knives cutting away at
her soul, her pride, her sense of dignity

Half healed wounds, open again never
given the time they need to heal

She obeys you

She takes orders well

But one day she's going to die

And your gonna realize she was the
best damn thing that this world ever had
to offer

And you lost her

"Golden Brown"

-H.B

24.

A dream

is a delicate

contradiction:

easily damaged,

difficult to destroy.

But lacking flesh,

its injuries are mine to bear.

Bruised by fear,

tenderness and stiffness

forbid movement

and freeze momentum.

Cut open by capitalism.

The blood only flows

away.

The weight

of "non-essentialism"

breaks my back.

But these wounds will heal.

Lacking flesh,

a dream

is more than mortal.

It nurtures me

until I am ready

to join it

in persisting.

www.ingramcontent.com/pod-product-compliance
Lightning Source LLC
LaVergne TN
LVHW011042200726
843509LV00011B/1333